# Steve Jobs

## The Life, Lessons & Rules For Success

### Influential Individuals

# Chapter One: A Confused Beginning

---

*"They were my parents 1000%." – Steve Jobs on his adoptive parents, Clara and Paul.*

*"They were my sperm and egg bank." – about his biological parents.*

---

A favorite childhood pastime for the future Apple boss was to tinker away in his garage with his adoptive father. It would be this tinkering – with friends rather than dad – a few years later that would lead to a creation that both changed the world and made Jobs rich beyond measure.

But that childhood could have been very different. Had it been so, who knows where the world might be today. Would we have the internet at our fingertips, on the go? Would our music be stored in a tiny box, a fraction the size of a CD? Steven Paul Jobs was born on February 24th 1955 to a Wisconsin student and her lecturer partner. Joanne Carole

Schieble's relationship with the young teacher was tempestuous; more on than off, and never especially stable. A part of that instability came from the fact that the relationship crossed racial lines. Her partner, Abdelfattah Jandali – better known as John – was of middle eastern descent. This kind of multi-cultural relationship was not well received in the US of the 1950's. It also failed to attract the support of John's family. The young man had become a political science teacher at the tender age of 23, and Carole was one of his students. They would go on to marry the year after Jobs was born, but at the time Carole fell pregnant, John felt that they lacked the maturity and financial security to enter into parenthood.

Frustrated, Carole headed to California and made arrangements for her child to be adopted. She was determined that he would go to a good home, and high up on the list of criteria she laid out was that his adopted parents would ensure he would go on to attend college. The couple Carole placed at the top of her list wanted a girl, but next in line were Paul and Clara Jobs. They would become parents to the new born baby. When Jobs became the world-famous business leader we know, John expressed an interest in meeting with his biological son. John claimed he did not realize he was going to be given to new parents, Steve was unrelenting in his rejection.

—

"I'd rather sell sh*t than meet with him", was Jobs' adult view of his biological father, a man he had, and would never, meet. Later, John and Carole would go on to have another child – a daughter they named Mona (who holds the dubious distinction of being the woman for whom Mona Simpson is named – Mona would later marry Simpsons' writer Richard Appel). As we shall see, Steve and Mona would get to know each other, and would develop a strong, close and deep bond. But that is many years in the future. Paul and Clara Jobs were an all-American couple, unable to have children of their own, but totally committed to the baby they adopted. Paul worked in Silicon Valley as a machinist. He was immensely creative; both a talented designer and outstanding manufacturer. The kind of man who might be described as being able to turn his hand to anything. He was a strong and stable role model to his young son.

That Jobs was adopted was never a secret to the child. But although he knew that out there somewhere he had other parents, they were this in name only. To young Steve Jobs, Clara and Paul were mom and dad – something that he would strongly defend throughout his life.

It is human nature to speculate. When somebody is outstandingly successful in their field, such as Steve, people try to offer reasons why. One such cause often pushed in Steve's direction is that he spent his life driven by the need to impress his biological parents. This is something he always denied. As he would often repeat, his parents were Clara and Paul Jobs – end of discussion.

When Steve was just two, his parents adopted a second child – a sister for the young boy, Patricia. This meant that the family home was no longer big enough, and they moved to a bigger house in Mountain View, California. Paul's love was to rebuild old cars, and in this new, larger home there was more room to indulge this passion. Little Steve was built his own workbench, and he would spend hours tinkering in the garage on old wrecks, echoing his father, learning skills and developing a passion for invention. He began to show a fascination for electronics, and an eye for taking a working part, and improving it. The seeds of his later life were firmly planted during those many hours helping his father. What was very clear, even in those early days, was that Steve Jobs possessed a huge capacity to learn and improve.

But like many such prodigies, while working one to one with somebody on something he loved was deeply motivating and satisfying, the more formal, restrictive rigors of school were something else entirely. We are also talking about the late 1950s and early 1960s, not a time in which the needs of the individual were especially recognized in our classrooms. Like so many very bright children, he quickly became bored. And with boredom, frustration and misbehavior followed.

Astonishingly, academic difficulties also started to appear. It was not that Steve lacked ability, just that to him the long winded, repetitive processes his teachers expected their pupils to follow offered not an iota of motivation. He preferred to find his own route to the answer, even if that meant making errors on the way.

In today's education system, such an approach may be encouraged, and recognized as evidence of outstanding ability. Half a century and more ago, such independence was to be squashed, at least in the school that Steve attended.

It was a sign of Paul and Clara's commitment to their son that they recognized the need for him to be challenged. The nearby area of Los Altos had a school system second to none, with a fine reputation for creative education. Unfortunately, Los Altos was also significantly up market compared to their Mountain View locality. Paul and Clara scraped together all the money they could, and moved to the region. At the age of twelve, they knew that Steve needed the challenge the schools there could offer if he was to achieve all he could from his considerable potential.

The move was an enormous success. Many of the families living in the region had fathers who were engineers, and some who specialized in electronics. Within a year, he got to know Bill Hewlett, the man behind Hewlett Packard, someone who also lived in Los Altos. Recognizing his talent and enthusiasm,

Bill offered him a summer job working for the company, even though he was still a young teenager.

The end of that summer saw Steve move schools and enter Homestead High School. It was there that he would meet another student who would go on to play a major part in his life. Homestead High School listed that student as a left field thinker, an electronics expert, a boy for whom the term 'Geek' might specially have been invented. That student was Steve Wozniak. The two would, of course, go on to form Apple. Steve Jobs was just thirteen at the time, the older Wozniak in his later teens.

But before Apple in the late 1960s, the protests against Vietnam are growing and young people are growing their hair, dabbling in drugs and dressing in ways that cause their parents to hold their heads in despair. The Beatles and the Stones are dominating world music and the Hippy culture is driving an interest in Eastern religions.

If you were to take a State in the US where the development of Youth Culture was at its strongest, that State could well be California. Steve Jobs was no different to many of his peers in this respect. He was attracted to the developing counterculture, in particular the teachings of far Eastern religion, especially Zen Buddhism. Like so many of the young people growing up around him, he wanted to be different. That was a desire he would hold throughout his life.

That determination to follow his own gut instinct, to follow the route he had chosen, is a lesson to all young entrepreneurs. Indeed, to all people who wish to make a difference. Follow your dreams, and you may just attain them. That was one of Jobs' mantras.

In his younger teens, that desire to be different frequently manifested itself in pranks, often played in conjunction with his friend, the 'geeky' Wozniak. Famously, on one occasion, the two invented a hack which allowed them to exploit the phone systems for international calls. With such freedoms, they decided to whom they would like to speak. They chose the Pope, and armed with youthful charm and wit, they set about contacting the Pontiff, making it all the way to his personal staff before being flagged. On another occasion, they rigged up a device which floated a large picture of a hand, middle finger raised, at a given cue. They decided to launch this invention during a formal graduation service. It did not go down well.

Wozniak being older than Jobs, left for the University of California when Jobs was sixteen. The two stayed in touch. Jobs frequently visited his older friend and was awe struck by the freedoms and liberalism of University life.

Steve spent some time working at the games manufacturer, Atari, where he worked as a technician. He managed to persuade his bosses that he would benefit from visiting India, and spent six months there, mostly learning about himself and religion.

Having experimented and experienced in the ways of many young people at the time, by his early twenties, Jobs had an idea of what he wanted to do. He loved innovating, taking something and making it better. He loved promoting his ideas, selling them using his charm and drive. He had a friend who was an electronics genius. All the ingredients were there. The Apple was about to be born.

# Chapter Two:  Bearing Fruit

---

*"You have to trust in something – your gut, destiny, life, karma, whatever. This approach has never let me down."*

---

At twenty-one, Steve Jobs still loved to play around in his garage. Not so much these days with his dad working together on old cars, but more with a couple of friends. Steve Wozniak was a couple of years older. The third member of the group, who he had met at Reeds College, was Ronald Wayne – slightly older still, and with the responsibilities of his own house and car.

The electronics whizz Wozniak led the inventing. And it was he who came up with their first computer. A do it yourself model, with all the parts showing. Although it looked a long way from the PCs we use today, the basic components of the home computer were there. A circuit board, which was to be linked to a keyboard and a monitor. There it was, the Apple 1. The three set up the company on 1st April 1976. It might have been April Fools' Day, but the company would not turn into any kind of joke. The three founders put up some money, persuaded a local dad to offer a small investment, and the company was born. Each member had their own principal role. Wayne was there to draft paperwork, design the branding and ensure that disagreements between the Steve's were resolved amicably and quickly; Wozniak was the designer, the inventor and Jobs would be the salesman, turning their ideas into dollars. In order to raise money, the Steve's (who had nothing) had sold possessions – a new pocket calculator for Wozniak and an old camper van for Jobs. Wayne was a little better off. But he soon began to fear for the company. Jobs' idea for funding was to beg, borrow and set everything off against future sales. It seemed a risky approach, and Wayne feared that if the company went bottoms up, it would be to him that creditors would flood. After all, when you have nothing - as was the case for the two Steve's - there was no point pursuing a debt, but if you owned a house and a car, then there were assets that could be sold or seized.

In a decision that he may have come to regret, although claims not, Wayne quickly divested himself of association with the company. He sold his share for $800 and left the organization. Financially, it was a poor decision, to understate in the strongest possible sense. Were he to sell today, his stake would be worth in the region of $75 billion. Still, we all make mistakes!

That left the two Steve's. They set a price on their original model of $666, claiming that the figure had no significance (666 being a number associated with the devil). Given their own impish wit, particularly in the early days of the business, the figure may well have held comic import. That cheeky, engaging, slightly on the edge wit stood them in good stead. They approached a local computer hardware store, called The Byte Shop, and put together a deal. Based on that single order, Jobs headed to an electronics supplier, Cramer, and managed to persuade the owner to a month's credit. The business model, if it can be called that, required that Wozniak could build enough computers and the byte shop could sell sufficient numbers to pay off the month's credit. Then it would get extended for the next thirty days.

The young men knew that they were onto something. There were other do it yourself computers out there, but none had really taken off. They were too complicated, and needed all kinds of add-ons to work. But that was Jobs' great genius, to take something and simplify it. Even today, look at Apple products, they still follow through on simplicity being paramount. It was he who persuaded Wozniak to reign in his naturally expansive urges, to create something that was simply a circuit to which a monitor and keyboard could be crudely attached, and leave it at that. It worked. That one outlet, the Byte Shop, sold over two hundred units of the

Apple 1 before the model was superseded. Find one of those original models, and you could expect to sell it for a quarter of a million dollars today. Not bad for something that cost a suspiciously specific price of $666.

A question often asked is: Why Apple? Many conspiracy theories exist. Was it a reference to that other great scientist and original thinker, Sir Isaac Newton? Wayne's original branding image would suggest that this could be the case. It was an ornate drawing of a man sitting under a tree, complete with apple ready to fall on him. Could it be homage to the Beatles, with their love of Eastern Religion and influence over youth culture, who of course produced their records on their Apple label?

Might it refer to Alan Turing? The great mathematician had been the mind behind solving the Enigma code during World War Two. Based at Bletchley Park, in the middle of England, he had led a team of code breakers to create a machine which could solve the codes German authorities were sending to their subs in the Atlantic. These codes would reveal the location of the great flotillas of vessels carrying essential goods from the US to the UK. Many believe that it was by solving these codes, and thus allowing the convoys to change direction and avoid their attackers, that the war was eventually won.

Turing was a national hero, but he was also homosexual, and

the two were not allowed to co-exist in post war Britain. He was arrested and chemically castrated, before losing all his access to secret information. However, between the war and this happening, he had designed the blue print for the electronic computer. It was never built. Shortly after his conviction and castration, he committed suicide (some suggest he was assassinated) through eating a poisoned apple.

But both Jobs and Wozniak deny that any of the above were behind the decision to call their business 'Apple'. It was much less complicated than this, they just wanted a simple, memorable icon from which to name the company. Keeping things simple is a lesson from which we could all learn. Within a few months, Wozniak had their computer's successor ready. The next Apple came to fruition in April 1977; it was distinctly upmarket compared to its elder brother, even having its own case. The enormous Commodore conglomerate was the market leader in those distant days, but the little Apple, its heredity gained from a garage workbench, was immediately a rival. It made use of color graphics, and storage was on cassette tape, but that soon was replaced by a floppy disk.

The computer had 64k of memory; a tiny amount by today's standards but back then, a more than decent amount. With a touch of blue sky thinking that would characterize the company through its life, and indeed still today, they eschewed the obvious name - 'Apple II', instead opting for the tricky to type 'Apple }{'.

But there were problems. Its integrated display unit and sixteen colors came at a price - one almost double the cost of the first model. In today's money, that is five and a half thousand dollars. A price beyond the personal computer market, a field very much in its infancy. And even for corporate sales, the price was high. Most businesses had their array of Commodores in any case.

Then came something that neither Steve Jobs nor Steve Wozniak could have predicted. That element of luck all entrepreneurs need if they are to break through the barrier that exists between a great idea and major commercial success. A student at the Harvard Business School, Dan Bricklin, was tinkering away at an idea. Something we take as so completely every day in the twenty first century that the thought of its origins rarely occurs to us. The computer spreadsheet.

Bricklin created, invented, originated - call it what you will - VisiCalc. And he wrote it using an Apple }{. The lack of a mouse (although it could be purchased separately) meant that the Apple was not the perfect device to run VisiCalc, but it was the best available.

The Steve's could not have invented a better program for their machine had they tried. It did not work on other computer systems; a way around the absence of a mouse (the computer came with a kind of games console trigger) was found; VisiCalc made computing a real tool for the workplace; and it was cheap. In fact, only a hundred dollars for the program. Suddenly, the highly specialized and expensive fields of bookkeeping and accounting became available to anybody – provided they owned an Apple. In a flash, the small company so recently working out of a garage, became a serious rival to the established brands – even the gigantic IBM was casting a wary eye over its shoulder.

By the end of the decade, just four years since three friends came up with the outrageous idea of building computers in a garage, the Apple }{ was a major world player. It was lightweight, had color graphics, came as a tidy unit, was easy to use, had VisiCalc. It was also built with the ability to expand. When more memory, or functionality, was needed, it could simply be added. There was no need to go and buy a completely new unit.

Over six million units were sold. And the brand was established. When VisiCalc was replaced, ultimately by the endemic Excel, new spreadsheets started life on Apple.

Jobs, and his friend Wozniak, were established.

# Chapter Three: The Birth of Macintosh

---

*"The only way to do great work is to love what you do."*

---

The Macintosh project marked a change in the fortunes of Apple founder Steve Jobs. By the onset of the 1980's, Apple was a popular target for outside investment, and had been turned into a public company. Jobs remained the boss, the man to turn to, but that status was just beginning to wobble, in the slightest, gentlest, jelly-like way.

The development of the Macintosh ran alongside the creation of another computer, affectionately known as the LISA. This acronym stood for Local Integrated System Architecture, although more than one commentator speculated that it was named after Jobs' illegitimate daughter, Lisa, (something he always denied) who he initially denied paternity for.

Initially, it was the Lisa that attracted most of Jobs' time. This was an expensive beast, costing more than a family car at $10000. Jobs, with his eye for simplification, saw that a mouse could easily be added to the Lisa which would make it even more user friendly. With his usual blunt single mindedness, Jobs set about the processes needed to add the tool.

But Apple was no longer a one or two-man show. Certainly, Jobs retained the creative and innovative lead for the company, but the corporate types that were moving in with their major investments were not unquestioning fans of the founder. They disliked his disregard for proper procedure; they did not warm to his often-abrasive approach. They were concerned by his youth.

We might add that they were limited by their past experiences.

Jobs cut corporate corners towards the development of the Lisa and it annoyed the Apple CEO, Michael Scott, and a major investor, Mark Markkula. They removed the founder from the Lisa project, and stripped him of his title of head of research and development. His role within the company was much reduced, his very powerful and infuential wings soundly clipped.

Jobs would not be denied a role in the company he had invented. He switched his attentions to the Macintosh (named after a type of Apple!), and set about improving this long-standing development project. He did what he did best. He took the product, simplified what he saw and made it more effective. That was what Jobs always did, and rarely did it fail to improve the project on which he was working.

The Lisa was ready for sale before the Macintosh, but made little impact in the commercial world. Apple set about producing a cheaper model, the Lisa II. Even that, at half the price of its older sister, failed to ripple the seas of computer use. The same could not be said for the Apple Macintosh. Jobs' adaptations, made against corporate wishes, revolutionized the product, redefined the market and moved Apple to the Number One position among computer manufacturers. Every time that Apple has hit the very highest highs, it has been because it innovated; because it took the norm and improved it. Those are the genes Steve Jobs pumped into his company. That determination to see through a project in which he believed, often against fierce opposition, is something from which everybody can take inspiration in their everyday, as well as professional, lives.

With competitors closing in on Apple's position in the market place, the launch of the Macintosh must have caused despair in board rooms across the globe.

We can see when we examine the development of the Macintosh in more detail, Jobs' classic footprint. The computer had been under the care of Jef Raskin, a talented developer. But Jobs usurped him. Not content to be just a figure head at his company, he gave all his considerable energy to the development of this computer.

He had recently been allowed a three-day tour (in exchange for shares in his company) to the electronics giant Xerox, and had left with some new ideas. He saw that the USP of the Macintosh would be its graphical user interface. In other words, the user would operate the computer through screens, or windows, rather than just through textual instructions. Using a graphical interface was simpler than controlling the computer with text; it was more intuitive; it was quicker. Think about how we operate our computers today – the notion of there not being separate screens, or windows, is incomprehensible. That is down to Jobs. He simply took the technology he was developing for Lisa, and adapted it for the Macintosh.

One of Jobs' strengths was his ability to recognize his own limitations and to take advantage of the talent surrounding him. He worked closely with another developer, Bud Tribble, on the computer. The final version that hit the market was not perfect. Its lack of a hard drive meant that the computer had to be started from a floppy disk, one that had to largely stay in place during the computer's operation. But this was more than compensated by the kind of graphics normally limited to the field of computers that costs thousands and thousands of dollars – the Macintosh was designed for the home market, and offered features unheard of in this sector.

The machine was simple and sleek. It contained many of the

ideas we take for granted today; the icons that show the computer is working, such as the watch which tells us programs are starting; it operated with multiple, overlapping windows. It was the modern computer.

At around $2500 dollars the early models were not cheap, and cost an additional $1500 dollars for the add-on drive that allowed easier additions to the computer. But nothing else came close to it in the home computing world.

The computer was ready for launch by 1984; and that specific year would prove to be the trigger for one of the most iconic, best known pieces of advertising in the history of that field. Apple hired sparkling young director Ridley Scott, riding on the crest of his Alien success. Naturally, he picked on themes from George Orwell's classic novel of State oppression, '1984', to promote the new Apple. Grey clad drones, shaved almost bald like the prisoners, are being lectured in a gigantic, featureless hall when a brightly dressed athlete bursts in, freeing them from their repression. It is an uplifting, stimulating advertisement, ground breaking in its way. It promotes youth, innovation and change.

At no point during the advertisement is the Apple Macintosh mentioned but at the end, the iconic Apple logo appears. The message is clear – Apple will free you from the oppression of your working drudge. It will open doors to a brighter future. As advertisements go, it was a huge success. 70,000 Apple

Macintosh computers were sold within three months of the machine hitting the market.

Within a year, Apple had also produced its first laser printer; capable of printing eight pages a minute. The printer was expensive, setting a buyer back several thousand dollars, but Apple had innovated another idea – this printer could be networked (officially, to 31 different work stations, but Apple itself ran forty machines to it at their headquarters. Another Jobs success. There were other laser printers on the market, but none that were as simple, usable and flexible. When that purchase price was divided by the number of computers the printer could support, the cost fell dramatically, to just around $150 – a very affordable sum for a business.

Almost overnight, Macintosh became the go to computer for small, medium and even some large businesses. Working with Adobe, shortly after this, the PageMaker software was launched, and the entire world of desktop publishing was at everybody's fingertips.

While commercially Jobs was at possibly his highest ever position, his role at Apple was becoming increasingly troubled. Jobs himself contributed to this. He was not the easiest person with whom to work. In actuality, he was a very difficult person to work for. Famously, he once sacked an entire team in a public meeting; he was quite capable of launching blistering attacks on his subordinates, verbally savaging them if their work was not of the impossibly high standards he set for himself. In board meetings, he said it as it was, often bruising some very large egos in the process. Egos of people who do not forget easily.

Jobs had a loyal following – we shall see that later – but he also had enemies. These enemies become more significant when we consider the corporate structure at Apple. Ask anybody not intimately connected to the company back in the middle to late 1980's and they would tell you that Apple and Steve Jobs were intractably linked. But, for all this, he was not CEO. He was still a young man, approaching thirty. Giant corporations did not put young men at their head; in turn, Michael Scott then Mark Markkula had been the CEO's of the firm. But Markkula had wanted only a short time with Apple, having already made one fortune, he wanted to enjoy the wealth he had accumulated. So, when he looked to step down, the Apple board decided on a senior executive working for Pepsi, John Sculley.

Initially Jobs was onside with this. Indeed, it was he who approached Sculley, famously asking: "Do you want to sell sugared water for the rest of your life? Or do you want to come with me and change the world?"

Sculley was impressed by the young entrepreneur with a growing reputation for making skilful innovations and reading the mood of the market place. A brief honeymoon period followed, but it did not take long for rifts to begin to form between the two.

Jobs' treatment of his employees was one of the first problems. Sculley felt it was unacceptable. Maybe it was, although the alternative view was that to work for Jobs was to be highly paid in a company that was clearly going places. Apple always came first for Jobs, and that may have been behind his inability to control his temper. Equally, he was still young and lacked the benefit of experience when it came to employee management skills. It must be said though that the calmer approach to his colleagues he displayed in later life produced largely better results. Everybody deserves respect – a truism Jobs maybe did not fully grasp at that point in his life.

Even back in the early days of the company, when three friends were getting together in Jobs' garage, Wayne described his friend and former partner as 'cold as an iceberg'. Sculley's approach was more collaborative, where the views of colleagues and underlings were more overtly welcomed. But a commercial problem also raised its head. That was the price to be set for the Macintosh. From the outset, Jobs felt it had to be an amount that made the machine affordable enough for the home user, as well as its corporate customers. He set a line in the sand at $1000. Sculley said that financially that figure was not viable for the company, and almost doubled Jobs' price. Then, just before it was due to hit the market, he added another $500 to the price.

After its initial surge of sales, interest in the Macintosh began to falter, perhaps because of the exceptionally high price. The Lisa was abandoned completely. Then, in March 1985, Sculley took away control of the Macintosh team from Jobs. The situation had started to get out of control. Jobs had wanted to slash the price of the computer, to jump start its sales. Sculley had his eyes on the returns to investors and would not contemplate such a move.

It was a stand-off – founder wanting to go one way, CEO determined to continue the set, but failing, path. It would come down to the board, and that meant no contest. Under no circumstances would these experienced, conservative businessmen back a volatile thirty something over their chosen CEO.

Once again Jobs displayed his inexperience. He tried to work behind the scenes to regain control of the Macintosh, confiding in the man who was in line to replace him as head of the team behind the computer. But Jean Louis Gassee felt his loyalty was to the board, and told Sculley of Jobs' sedition. He informed the CEO that Jobs was planning a takeover, although it seems somewhat strange to take over what was your own company. Except, of course, Apple had now been partially subsumed by its investors, and the fine details meant that it was no longer Jobs' company.

The shootout happened at the next board meeting. It was an occasion that might best be described as a little awkward. Sculley asked Jobs outright if he planned to remove him as CEO. Jobs confirmed that this was indeed his motivation. Sculley asked the board for their views. Once again, it was he that they backed.

Sculley, knowing that this confrontation had been inevitable, had his plans well formed. He restructured the management of the company. He promoted Gassee and made Jobs Chairman, little more than an honorary role.

It was anathema to a man like Steve Jobs, somebody who wanted to be at the center of all that happened, to be a hands-on manager, not a desk bound corporate type. Soon after the meeting, he resigned, a decision that would prove to be fateful for Apple and its ambitions.

# Chapter Four: What Came NeXT?

---

*"Sometimes life hits you in the head with a brick. Don't lose faith."*

*"The great thing is that Apple's DNA hasn't changed."*

---

When Jobs set out on his next enterprise, he took many key Apple staff with him. He might have been a difficult man to work with, but his success engendered enormous loyalty from those with whom he worked closest.

He created NeXT, which set out to build prestigious computers that would underpin the work of institutions such as government bodies and Universities. The first model took three years to develop, and was unveiled in 1988. The main reason for the length of period prior to the launch was litigation from Apple, which claimed that Jobs and his new team had stolen their secrets, pilfering their technology.

But the system was worth waiting for. Its processors were of the Ferrari kind, and the software it ran was more than a challenge to Apple and PC at the time. Over the next few years NeXT was continuously upgraded. Delivered in a stunning black box, the sleek machine developed a CD ROM drive, a fast color printer, improved color and so forth. The next stage of the operation, with hardware at such a high standard, was to work on software development. Jobs took his company to Intel, joined forces and set about taking NeXT and its models to even higher peaks.

Meanwhile, Apple experienced a brief upsurge – the markets felt that without the conflict with Jobs, Sculley could get on with running the company undistracted. But they lost sight of their USP. The point about Apple was that their computers were simple, they were flexible, and they appealed not just to the 'geeks' but to the everyday user. The company, under Gassee's influence, put its energy into taking the Macintosh upmarket, with the introduction of the Macintosh II. This would be an expensive machine, selling fewer models than its predecessor, but at a far higher profit margin. The success of this venture was debatable, at best.

They also made the corporate error of feeling that they could take their eye off the everyday user market, they thought that they had this under control. But by 1990 their supremacy had been challenged, and then surpassed. IBM had duplicated many of the benefits of Apple machines, but at a fraction of the cost. Apple had established a loyal and tolerant customer base, but without Jobs' innate sense of what worked, even they were beginning to consider different manufacturers. Their position was not helped by the fact that Microsoft had its own graphical user interface ready and raring to go, Windows Version Three. Apple put its energy behind ClarisWorks, a perfectly acceptable word processing program which many readers will recall; but Word was always going to be more successful. And Apple had allowed itself to diversify by selling numerous different models.

Simplicity, that was the Apple way under Jobs. It was a term that could no longer be applied to the company. Customers simply did not know what to buy, so they kept their wallets closed. The company who had produced one of the greatest advertisements of all time to launch the original Macintosh, then produced a long (30 minutes), tedious and old-fashioned critical advertising film which spent as much time doing down the competition as promoting its own products. Customer satisfaction, already faltering, hit new depths. Apple tried a short lived and unsuccessful liaison with Motorola and IBM. But nothing seemed to work. In the end, it faced up to the fact that its attempts to build a new operating system to make it competitive once more, were failing.

It decided to hop on to an external provider. It short-listed two; ironically both companies run by former Apple employees. Jean Louis Gassee had left Apple some years previously and set up BeOS; the other system had been developed by none other than NeXT. It was clearly the better choice and Apple opted for it. Not only did it buy the product, but the entire company, which meant that its founder was once more on board. Steve Jobs was back at Apple.

His interests were diversifying as he got older and more experienced. Despite this, he retained the off-beat approach of the maverick. Many might argue genius the correct term. To put one of his other ventures in context, we need to step back a little. George Lucas is the man behind such successful film franchises as Star Wars and Indiana Jones. His success had allowed him to produce his own production company, which he called Lucasfilm. But by 1986, Lucasfilm could do with a cash injection. With Jobs hanging around in Limbo – NeXT being in dispute with Apple over the legality or otherwise of its technology – the computing genius put his hands in his deep pockets. Lucasfilm was an odd mix; it included developing computer hardware and selling graphics systems to various agencies such as medical companies and also vested towards government interests.

The hardware business was called Pixar, and Jobs bought it. The company provided a distraction for Jobs, and a much-needed cash injection for Lucasfilm. But then NeXT got the go ahead and Jobs turned his attention back to his first love. Pixar floundered on, and within four years was only half the size as when Jobs bought it. At the point of near termination for Pixar, one of its staff, John Lasseter, came up with the idea of making a series of short advertisements for the company's hardware. It was a last ditch attempt to save an ailing business. Crucially, although he did not at this stage realize the importance, they would be animations.

The hardware side of the business was beyond recovery and Jobs sold it, but he was very interested with the computer driven animations. Once again, we have an example of Jobs at his best. The computer animation was already in place; the skills were there in the company. It was perhaps that they were just producing the wrong material. Working with Lasseter, he suggested a cartoon film, aimed at the general public. Pixar reached an agreement with Disney, and *Toy Story* was born. The rest, as they say, is history. Of course, there was much more to *Toy Story* than great animation; the film changed the way cartoons worked. Jobs, Lasseter and their team realized that although their target audience was small children, they would be taken to the cinema by adults. And those older people would welcome some entertainment as well. The concept of the cartoon which operates for young children at one level, with humor for the adults at another, was born.

Pixar went on to win, by the time of Steve Jobs' death, no

fewer than an astonishing twenty-six academy awards. And it was Disney's decision to purchase Pixar in 2006 that turned Steve Jobs from very comfortable, to a billionaire several times over. He also became the largest shareholder in the Disney corporation. John Lasseter was rewarded for his work and foresight by being made head of animation at Pixar, then Disney itself. He said of Jobs:

*"He saw the potential of what Pixar could be before the rest of us, and beyond what anyone ever imagined."*

*"Steve took a chance on us and believed in our crazy dream of making computer animated films; the one thing he always said was to simply 'make it great'."*

Sometimes, taking a chance is the best way to reap rewards. Jobs not only diversified his interests but was a success at almost everything he did. Since Jobs' departure from Apple, the company had experienced challenging times. It was not on the edge of bankruptcy, far from it. It was still a leading player in the world of technology, but its previous primacy had been usurped; now it was in the chasing bunch, no longer setting the pace for innovation.

Jobs was away from the company for twelve years. One and a half million shares, along with nearly half a billion dollars was the price Apple paid to get the NeXT operating system, the company and its founder back.

But there was no immediate fix, perhaps surprisingly given

Jobs' reputation. The company's founder set about the business with his usual clarity of thought and vision. Firstly, he decided that the Company's CEO, Gil Amelia, needed to move on. The board agreed, and tried to convince Jobs to take over the role. He was now of an acceptable age to the corporate mind! But Jobs was also committed to the growing power that was Pixar, and decided he could not commit to both positions. He agreed to take on the role of temporary CEO at Apple.

Next he reverted to his business mantra – simplicity. He realized that one of Apple's problems was that it had too many products in the computer field. He slashed the myriad options, leaving the company with just four – two for business and two primarily for home use.

He cut swathes through the numerous licensing deals in which the company had become involved, and either sold or closed many of Apple's subsidiaries. The impact was that Apple's operating system was now just three per cent of the entire market. However, that three per cent was 100% Apple. The stock market was uncertain; it held its breath for a moment, exhaled, and decided to place its trust in Steve Jobs. The company's competitors could not believe their luck. They felt that Jobs had cut his company's throat, and sent it to its death. As we now know, when we enter an Apple Store with its 'floating' glass staircases and immaculately presented goods (both holding Jobs' signature), they were being somewhat presumptuous in doubting the ability of the new CEO. Michael Dell, of Dell Computing, risked ending up with egg on his face when he said the following about Apple's approach at a conference:

"What would I do? I'd shut it down and give the money back to the shareholders."

The jibe must have hit home, because a decade later, when Apple was once again securely ensconced at the top of the electronics tree and the most valuable company in the world; Jobs sent the following email to his employees:

"Team, it turned out that Michael Dell wasn't perfect at predicting the future. Based on today's stock market close, Apple is worth more than Dell," he wrote. "Stocks go up and down, and things may be different tomorrow, but I thought it was worth a moment of reflection today."

Maybe a chip on his shoulder was another of Jobs' ingredients towards his recipe of success.

Another major move that Jobs initiated to restore Apple's place in the hierarchy was one that would have seemed impossible only a short time before. Microsoft was now the big boy in the playground, and it was not a friend of Apple. The number of disputes over patents, lawsuits over ownership of technology and so forth had turned the two into enemies. But as we saw earlier, Jobs always placed Apple first. He saw that if his baby was to regain its former glory, some kind of a deal with Microsoft had to be found. The deal was brokered, enemies repaired their differences and Apple took another leap forwards. Even Microsoft founder Bill Gates bought into the plans.

A further issue that was a cause of concern to Jobs was security around the company's developments. He instituted what many saw as Draconian measures to ensure that secrets stayed within the doors of the corporation, chasing former employees around the world if they were suspected of breaking the terms of their contracts and leaking to competitors of the press. He went as far as to hang a mock-up of a world war two poster which said: 'Loose Lips Might Sink Ships'. In other words, employees, leak at your peril.

Within a year of his return to Apple two new products were released. The Power Mac and the Power Book were innovative, intuitive, brilliantly packaged and immensely popular. Apple customers breathed a sigh of relief, and flooded back to their previously first choice supplier. In 1998, another change in direction saw Apple climb another rung towards ascendency; the iMac hit the shelves, a computer designed for the internet.

The iMac was another innovation which destroyed an established aspect of the computing market place, in a similar way to how the Macintosh had ended the days of text operations. It had no floppy disk drive, and within two years that method of booting up and adding software would disappear completely from all new machines.

A year later and the iBook became available. And with that, Wi-Fi technology hit the world through Apple's AirPort base station. It is not overstating the point to say that Apple had taken the idea of personal computing, turned it upside down, and shaken out the old and the redundant. At the turn of the Millennium, Jobs ended his position as temporary CEO and agreed to take on the position full time.

At this point, another piece of Jobs' genius came to the fore. Major manufacturers were considering the impact of the internet on personal computing. The over-arching consensus was that personal computing would soon be redundant, that the hardware would simply be a tool to allow the internet to dominate users' experiences. But Jobs saw things differently. He took a wider view. Yes, the internet was becoming ever more dominant, on-line activity prevailing in much of people's lives. But other changes were happening, and those were in the field of digital provision.

Jobs had the foresight to see that the personal computer might adapt to another role. Yes, it would be the way to access the all-pervading internet, but it could also become a hub for the growth of digital facilities. Like all successful entrepreneurs, Jobs understood the importance of moving with the times. For

Jobs, as well as moving with the times, he also set them. With varying degrees of success, Jobs led Apple to the development of its digital arm. iMovie came first, and it was not a great success; the chance to make one's own films using only an Apple computer did not set the world on fire, but other innovations did.

iTunes hit the market in 2002, and has, as we know, dominated the music market ever since. iDVD and iPhoto were among early iInnovations as well. A huge development was then just around the corner. The iPod revolutionized the way we accessed our music. The advertising slogan for this little gem was: 'A thousand songs in your pocket'; no longer would we need to jog carefully while our music jumped about on our Walkman, or carry a Ghetto Blaster on our shoulder, announcing our taste in music to an uninterested and frankly (justifiably) annoyed world.

Whether the iPod is the biggest success of Apple is now open to question; perhaps the iPad is bigger – once again a tool that revolutionized the way we accessed the internet. Perhaps even bigger is the iPhone, ubiquitous and subject to numerous (many would say inferior) copies, the little hand-held tool has changed the way we live our lives.

The point about Apple is that under Steve Jobs, it was always where it needed to be when change was on the horizon…and more often than not, he was the instigator of that change.

# Chapter Five:  Private Person

---

*"Being the richest man in the cemetery doesn't matter to me."*

---

We have considered in great detail Steve Jobs the corporate genius. We have seen him lead Apple from nothing to the biggest player in the computing world not once, but twice; we have seen him create a new company that would eventually save his original baby; we have even seen him revolutionize the animated film world, and take over as the largest shareholder in the giant woolly mammoth that is Disney.

But what of the man? We know that he could be volatile in the work place, that sometimes his single-minded drive frustrated, perhaps even scared, those who didn't match his expectations. But there is another side to Steve Jobs. A personal one that is kept much quieter. One in which he sought to keep out of the public eye as much as was possible for somebody regarded by many as a Guru.

As we saw in the opening chapter, Jobs was an adopted child, given away in a planned event by his biological mother, potentially without the full knowledge of his father. We know that he never sought to meet his biological father, and that he rebuffed any requests to meet. But Jobs did have a biological sister, and the two were close. He and Mona would spend much time together and she became a confidante. An advisor on matters close to Steve Jobs' heart.

Jobs also fathered a child with a fellow student, Chris Ann Brennan. Apple was still a fledgling company at the time, and for a while Jobs denied all responsibility for the child, Lisa. He said that he was infertile, and so the girl could not be his. However, later tests insisted upon by Chris Ann Brennan proved that he was the father, and from that moment he took his responsibilities seriously. He provided proper financial support to the struggling mother, but also established a close bond with his daughter. Chris Ann and Steve Jobs had an off-on relationship throughout the 1970s, although she later claimed, in her book *The Bite in the Apple* that Jobs was difficult. She said that on telling him he was going to be a father that he offered a 'fiery' look and left the house without another word. As Apple grew, he possessed a sense of entitlement that made him a very difficult person with which to live. She also said that he could be sexist, but that he had developed these tendencies following his trip to India in 1974. That excursion had seemed life changing for Jobs. Not only had he returned home smelling and parasite ridden, but he had developed an understanding of the madness of Western Industrialization. According to Brennan the change in his personality was not beneficial. She described him, on his return to the US, as a 'bewildered, lunatic Shaman,' and a 'fully fledged sexist bully'.

She alleged that he made statements like 'women felt pain in child birth as a punishment for their sins'. However, such sexism did not extend to his daughter, and they lived together for a number of years when she was younger.

Jobs' love life was complex. He dated the singer Joan Baez briefly, and the two stayed friends throughout his life. Indeed, Baez was one of the last people to talk with him before his premature death. When she asked him, close to death, what it had been like to change the world, he answered (with great understatement) 'OK'. He dated a friend, Tina Redse, for a long time, and even proposed to her. But she did not accept, and soon their relationship dwindled.

He was giving a talk at the Stanford Business School in 1989 when he came across an attractive and intelligent student. Laurene Powell was a blond, independent thinker – militant, vegan and possessed a razor-sharp mind.

Jobs was besotted, and sought the advice of his sister. He told Mona, in a gabbled stream of consciousness, that he had met a girl, she was beautiful, intelligent and had a dog. He went on like a teen with his tongue hanging out until he determined, there and then, to marry her.

Two years later the deed was done. A Buddhist ceremony marked the marriage, which was led by Kobun Chino Otogawa, a Zen monk of Jobs' acquaintance.

Within six months their first child, Reed (a son) was born, and soon Erin and Eve would follow. The birth of his children led to Jobs putting up even more a screen around his private life. We know that he was a follower of minimalism. The ex-Apple CEO John Sculley once visited his home, to find an expensive, ornate lampshade, a chair, a bed and a fine piece of art, but nothing more. Perhaps this was the influence of his experiences in India, which made him eschew consumerism. His beliefs can be seen to be echoed in the packaging for Apple products, which show the clean lined simplicity of a minimalist approach to life.

Jobs was an extremely rich man, although little is known about his charitable work. He once, famously, cut all of Apple's charitable donations, but at the same time it is believed that he contributed widely to many causes, especially those which supported sufferers from cancer. It is known that much of the $10 billion he left in his will has been used to support many good causes. Laurene, his wife for twenty years prior to his death, contributes much from the wealth he created.

But there is a lesson there for us all, especially in the social

---

44

media driven world in which we now live. Keep a bit of privacy, a touch of secrecy about your life. There will be times, just as there were for Jobs in his last days (and perhaps even when business was especially rough) when we all need a quiet, private place into which we can cozy up. Jobs, as we can see, can teach us about more in life than just business.

# Chapter Six: The End of a Life

---

*"Death is very likely the single best invention of Life. It is Life's change agent."*

*"Remembering that you are going to die is the best way I know to avoid the trap of thinking you have something to lose."*

---

In 2003, things were looking rosier than ever. Pixar was an enormous success, Apple was at the top of its game and personally he had a loving wife and family. Then he fell ill. The problem appeared to be abdominal, and following a series of investigations, it was discovered that he had a tumor in his pancreas.

Pancreatic cancer is one of the more serious forms, especially over a decade ago. But Jobs retained his belief in the teachings of the East, and sought out alternative treatments for his condition. However, none proved to offer much improvement. Finally he decided to resort to more mainstream treatments, and an operation was organized. Jobs told his employees that he had the condition, but in an unusual and treatable form. They were not to worry.

He told them that the operation was a success, and he needed neither radiotherapy nor chemotherapy, that his tumor was gone, and it would not be coming back.

But, as is often the case with cancer of the pancreas, his optimism proved to be short lived and the condition did return. Following a period of recovery, he seemed back to his energetic, determined, committed best until he gave the keynote speech at the Apple Computer Worldwide Developers' Conference in 2006. Concerns were raised – the man who was Apple did not appear his normal, focused self; he seemed distracted, and his speech was lacking energy and pace. It was not at all what the attendees had come to expect. Rumors circulated; some believed that he had lost his enthusiasm for the company, and was going to step down once more. Others felt that he was unwell. Those within the company who controlled media releases were clear, though. 'Steve's health is robust,' they claimed. Perhaps a little too fervently.

Then stories began to leak; one told of his original cancer, and that he had waited for nine months until having it treated. Others that he was once again suffering from cancer. When he appeared in 2008, the public saw a man who had lost his solidity, who looked thin and weak, and on whom the trademark black polo neck sweater hung like loose skin on a person who had dieted far too vigorously.

In the end, some kind of statement had to be forthcoming. Near the start of 2009, it was announced to Apple employees that Jobs was suffering from a type of hormonal imbalance, and it was that which was impacting upon his health. But many began to fear the truth. A liver transplant followed, and once again the news was put out that he was recovering well and would soon be back to work.

He continued, increasingly out of the public eye, until finally in June 2011 a statement was issued by Apple which announced that Steve Jobs would be taking leave of absence for an indefinite period.

Jobs added to the announcement, saying: "I love Apple so much and hope to be back as soon as I can. In the meantime, my family and I would deeply appreciate respect for our privacy." A month or two later, he resigned as CEO of Apple, and people knew that something deeply serious was wrong. The end came quickly, and on October 5th 2011, at just 56 years of age, Steve Jobs died.

Few people have genuinely changed the world. That is something that can be said about Steve Jobs. Computers have altered our lives, mostly for good; the internet, digital technology and so forth make life easier, communication is faster and information more available. Some point out the negatives, the loss of social skills and relationships; the ease with which hate can spread and misery induced.

But those negatives are not the fault of Steve Jobs. He provided the opportunity; how we seek to use it is down to us. What Jobs gave us was access to the latest technology, and an intuitive, easy way to access it. In many ways he made society, indeed the world, more equal. Information and knowledge are more easily shared; they are available instantly in many forms. Technology allows us to see relatives in far off lands, keeps us in touch with friends and family.

Even without their leader and inspiration, Apple has gone on to further success. Under the current boss, Tim Cook, profits have more than doubled, share price has increased. There are more Apple Shops than ever, and more employees. But that is all down to the foundations Jobs laid, not once, but twice.

It is impossible to say where we would be today without Steve Jobs – perhaps somebody would have stepped into his shoes and our lives would not be much different. But somebody had to break the mold, bring technology to the masses, and that man was Steve Jobs.

His legacy? He changed the world. It doesn't come much bigger than that.

*"Stay hungry, stay foolish."*

# Chapter Seven: Rules for Success

Though Steve Jobs has passed away, his legacy will be with us forever. Steve was undoubtedly a very successful entrepreneur. Here are ten life lessons about success that we can learn from the man:

## Rule #1.  Anticipate the future

Steve Jobs once quoted ice hockey legend Wayne Gretzky, saying:

"I skate to where the puck is going to be, not where it has been."

This quote has been evident throughout Steve's working life. Instead of releasing products on a par with the current marketplace, Jobs designs and creates products using his ability to anticipate future trends. The iPhone has revolutionized the phone industry and digital music sales have now completely overtaken the now ancient "CD".

This method of thinking is a great way to ensure your product or service stands out from the crowd. Creativity is key. Many people believe that creativity is an innate ability, blessed only for the lucky few. Jobs likes to simplify it: "Creativity is connecting things." This means seeking inspiration from a variety of industries. He has found inspiration in a phone book, visiting India, Zen meditation, a food processor at Macy's, and at The Four Seasons hotel chain. Jobs doesn't "steal" ideas as much as he uses ideas from other industries to inspire his own creativity.

## Rule #2.  Do what you love

"Your work is going to fill a large part of your life, and the only way to be truly satisfied is to do what you believe is great work. And the only way to do great work is to love what you do. If you haven't found it yet, keep looking. Don't settle. As with all matters of the heart, you'll know when you find it." It's age old advice, but for good reason. Jobs has stuck to doing what he truly loves his entire life and this he believes, makes all the difference. It is difficult to stay motivated and inspired in the same field year after year unless you have a serious passion for it. This is the key to good work according to Jobs.

# Rule #3.  Don't fear failure

After being fired from his own company in 1984, Jobs had this to say about the situation at a commencement speech in 2005 at Stanford University:

"I didn't see it then, but it turned out that getting fired from Apple was the best thing that could have ever happened to me. The heaviness of being successful was replaced by the lightness of being a beginner again, less sure about everything. It freed me to enter one of the most creative periods of my life."

What can we learn from this? We should not fear failure as it isn't the end of the road. Failure is an opportunity to learn. To fall back and prepare more thoroughly for the next shot. If failure is only ever viewed in this way, success is inevitable.

# Rule #4.  Sell dreams, not products

Steve Jobs did not sell computers; he built tools to unleash human potential.

To Jobs, customers are never just "consumers." They are people with hopes, dreams and ambitions.  He builds products to help people achieve their dreams.  He once said, "some people think you've got to be crazy to buy a Mac, but in that craziness we see genius."

View your customers in this light and the quality of your output will improve dramatically. Help someone unleash their inner potential and you will have a customer for life. Customers tend to trust individuals who are serious about what they do, and willing to take the time to achieve a deep understanding of their craft. Take the time every day to learn more about your customers, their industry and their challenges.

## Rule #5.  Focus on the positive

As we know, Steve Jobs was an adopted child. He could have easily taken the route many adopted children do and rebelled in life, going down the wrong road especially in his teenage years.

However, young Steve Jobs kept focusing on the positive: he was thankful for his loving adoptive parents, he also found a positive channel (technology and computer) to pour his energy into, and in the end we all know what he achieved. You too, can benefit from the power of positive thinking. If you are the kind of person who often sees the glass as half-empty, try to start focusing on the positive things in your life and what you already have. An attitude of gratitude is essential to a happy life.

## Rule #6.  Say no to 1,000 things

"People think focus means saying yes to the thing you've got to focus on. But that's not what it means at all. It means saying no to the hundred other good ideas that there are. You have to pick carefully. I'm actually as proud of the things we haven't done as the things I have done. Innovation is saying no to 1,000 things."

Jobs thinks differently about design. Simplicity is the ultimate sophistication. This simplicity stretches further than just the product. It is in the packaging, the Apple stores, the advertisements. Focus only on what truly matters and ignore the rest. Innovation means eliminating the unnecessary so that the necessary may speak.

## Rule #7.  Become comfortable with risk.

Jobs and Wozniak ran out of money while developing the first Apple computer. Instead of giving in, Jobs sold his van and Wozniak sold his graphing calculator. Where there's a will, there's a way.

Learn to see obstacles as opportunities in disguise. Once you do that, there will always be ways to overcome those obstacles.

Even when Apple had become a huge success, Jobs was still willing to take big risks. He even decided to cannibalize his company's products in the name of progress. Many CEOs would have been hesitant to develop the iPhone, knowing full well that it would help to make the iPod obsolete – but Jobs did it anyway (and took a big bite out of the lucrative mobile market).

Most of the time, we need to take risks in order to move forward. Just be careful and make sure that the risk that you took was a calculated risk. Think thoroughly, weigh the best and worse case scenarios of an action against each other, and then you can decide whether the risk is worth taking.

## Rule #8.  Surround yourself with great people

Not only did Steve Jobs have Steve Wozniak as a partner, he also worked with Johny Ive, Tim Cook, and John Lasseter (Pixar CCO). Steve Jobs wasn't able to achieve the success he achieved on his own, it all comes down to a team effort. Through choosing such talented co-workers, this has enabled Jobs to create massive success with not only Apple, but also

Pixar.

The people you surround yourself with are the people that will shape your future. If you surround yourself with smart, hard working people that share your vision, then you are much more likely to achieve it. You are the average of the five people you spend most of your time with, so choose wisely.

## Rule #9.   Master your message

Steve Job's was arguably the world's greatest corporate storyteller. Product launches became an art form, a presentation that people could actually become excited about. You may have the most innovative idea in the world but if you cannot elicit emotion towards it, it doesn't matter. Think differently about your story. Explain what you are and who you are. This will ensure your customers know what you stand for.

## Rule #10.  Remember you'll be dead soon

"Remembering that I'll be dead soon is the most important tool I've ever encountered to help me make the big choices in life. Because almost everything — all external expectations, all pride, all fear of embarrassment or failure – these things just fall away in the face of death, leaving only what is truly important."

When you are confused, scared, embarrassed, or anything, just remember that you'll be dead soon. Face your mortality daily as a constant reminder, life is short; make it count.

"When I was 17, I read a quote that went something like: 'If you live each day as if it was your last, someday you'll most certainly be right.' It made an impression on me, and since then, for the past 33 years, I have looked in the mirror every morning and asked myself: "If today were the last day of my life, would I want to do what I am about to do today?" And whenever the answer has been "No" for too many days in a row, I know I need to change something."

# Chapter Eight: Steve Jobs; A Life in 44 Facts

Steve Jobs was adopted shortly after being born.

Biologically, Jobs was half Arab. His biological father was Syrian and his mother was American.

Jobs biological parents had one request - that Jobs be adopted by two college-educated people. The biological parents found out that neither Clara nor Paul Jobs had ever graduated from college, but the adoption went through when it was promised that Steve Jobs would receive a university education.

Jobs was bullied in the sixth grade for allegedly being odd. This resulted in him giving his parents an ultimatum - he would drop out of school if they didn't move. So, they moved to Los Altos in California (the birthplace of Apple) where he met fellow engineer Bill Fernandez, who introduced him to Apple's co-founder Steve Wozniak.

Jobs met Steve Wozniak in high school--Wozniak was 18 and Jobs was just 13.

Jobs was a pescetarian, which meant he ate no meat except fish.

Jobs dropped out of college, but continued his education by informally auditing classes.

Fortunately, one class he decided to audit was a calligraphy course. Although he didn't realize it at the time, this course would play a big part in Jobs' future and the look of Apple. This is especially relevant to the attention Apple places on font and typography.

At this point Jobs was struggling to get by. He would sleep on friends' floors and would return Coke bottles for money. He would also survive off free meals from the local Hare Krishna temple.

His GPA was hardly impressive – just 2.65. The structure of school learning wasn't suited to Jobs as he preferred to learn in unconventional ways.

On his seven-month trip to India, Jobs experimented with LSD and would eventually adopt the practices of Zen Buddhism.

"One of the two or three most important things I have done in my life." What could Jobs be referring to? Surprisingly, his experimentation with LSD.

Early on in the business, Jobs stole from his co-founder and partner Steve Wozniak. When the pair first created the Breakout game for Atari, they planned on splitting the pay 50-50. Although Atari gave Jobs $5,000 for the game, Jobs told Wozniak they got $700, leaving Wozniak to take home $350 while Jobs pocketed the other $4,650.

When working at Atari, he would walk around barefoot and rarely showered. This prompted complaint from his colleagues and he was moved to the night shift.

Apple's first logo was actually created by the third founder, Ronald Wayne. Ronald's only real claim to fame today is that he sold his 10 percent stake after just two weeks for $800. Today that 10% would be worth over $75 billion.

The original Apple I computer was priced at $666.66. There are two main theories as to why. Firstly, Devil worship. Secondly, this was exactly one third more than the wholesale cost of $500. I'll let you choose your preference!

Jobs was fired from the company he built in 1985. Despite the initial anger, he later recognized the situation as a blessing in disguise. This gave him the chance to experiment creatively and purchase an animation studio, which would later be known as Pixar.

Shortly after being shown the door at Apple, he applied to fly on the Space Shuttle as a civilian astronaut. After being rejected he then even considered starting a computer company in the Soviet Union.

When Jobs was 23, he had a child called Lisa Brennan. For years he denied paternity, claiming the child wasn't his. Eventually Jobs accepted responsibility and accepted Lisa has his own. He eventually changed her name to Lisa Brenna-Jobs. Despite initially denying paternity, around the time Lisa was born, Jobs named a new Apple computer the Apple Lisa (although Jobs claimed it simply stood for Local Integrated

Software Architecture).

Even though Jobs denied paternity, at around the time Lisa was born Jobs named a new Apple compute the Apple Lisa. He claims this actually only stood for Local Integrated Software Architecture but it seems a bit of a coincidence.

Jobs annual salary at Apple was always $1. Nevertheless, with the shares he owned in Apple and Pixar he was hardly struggling.

Jobs grew very close with his biological sister, Mona Simpson, after they made contact with each other later in life. They shared much in common and both were artistic.

Mona wrote a book which was eventually turned into a movie called "Anywhere But Here". The film was dedicated to Steve Jobs.

Jobs was hardly the philanthropist. He cut Apple's philanthropic efforts in the early days of the company, stating they would return once profits went up. Profits certainly went up over the years, but the philanthropy never returned.

Jobs had an entire team devoted to packaging who studied the experience of opening a box to learn how to achieve the excitement and emotional response that is now common with Apple products.

Known to be a bit of a hothead, Jobs held a position on Fortune's list of America's toughest bosses.

On Fortune's list of America's most admired companies,

Apple has previously been ranked number one.

Jobs wanted complete control on Apple's perception by the public. Apple even went so far as to sue teenager Nicholas Ciarelli for his Think Secret blog, where he revealed rumors and secret details about upcoming Apple products.

He is listed as either primary inventor or co-inventor for 346 United States patents related to a range of technologies, with most of the patents being for design.

Jobs had romantic relationships with Joan Baez and Diane Keaton.

Steve Wozniak claims that Jobs never actually learned how to code.

Jobs was once invited to spend the night in the Lincoln bedroom of the White House by Bill Clinton.

"I'd rather sell dog shit than PCs," is a quote attributed to Jobs and his severe dislike for PCs.

Jobs would take advantage of a loophole which allowed him to legally drive around in his silver Mercedes without ever needing plates. How did he manage this? California has a rule that a car owner has six months to put plates on a new car. Jobs just changed cars (to the identical model) every six months, allowing him to drive without plates.

It has been said that he would often park in spots reserved for the handicapped at Apple headquarters.

What color immediately comes to mind when you think of

Apple? I'm sure it is white. Jobs originally did not want the color white near any of his Apple products until he had his mind changed after an introduction to the "moon gray" shade. Larry Page and Sergey Brin, the two Google founders, had the fortune of having Steve Jobs as a mentor. He would even share some of his advisors with the pair.

When Google created its Android devices and entered into competition with Apple, Jobs was furious.

It was 2003 when Jobs discovered he had pancreatic cancer. He opted for non-traditional medicine at first including acupuncture, herbal remedies, a vegan diet and even consulted a psychic. The doctor had recommended an immediate operation. He eventually opted for traditional medicine after 9 months and went in for surgery.

Some are of the opinion that waiting 9 months to enter surgery could have cost Steve Jobs his life.

When Jobs died, Disney World, Disneyland and all the Apple and even Microsoft properties flew their flags at half-staff.

Jobs is buried in an unmarked grave. His last words? "Oh wow, oh wow, oh wow,".

Tim Cook revealed in a 2014 interview that Jobs main office and nameplate are still as they were in 2011, when Jobs passed away.

Steve Jobs Day is October 16th, 2011.

# Conclusion

Only a select few individuals can claim to have changed the world. Steve Jobs is one of these. He may be gone but he's not forgotten. The mythology around the man is so strong that even five years after his death he still dominates online discussion, more popular than Tim Cook (Apple's current CEO), the Tesla and SpaceX CEO, Elon Musk, Facebook's CEO, Mark Zuckerberg, and the Microsoft founder, Bill Gates– according to Google Trends. I'll leave you with one last story that sums up the man that was Steve Jobs.

It was back in January 2008 and Vic Gundotra was working at Google. Just before Apple launched the App Store and the iPhone 3GS, Jobs was preparing his Macworld San Francisco keynote where he would show off web apps for the iPhone and custom home screen bookmarks. Jobs had found something he wasn't happy about with Google's web app. He promptly called Gundotra who was at church. When Gundotra got round to calling Jobs back, the conversation went as follows:

*"Hey Steve – this is Vic", I said. "I'm sorry I didn't answer your call earlier. I was in religious services, and the caller ID said unknown, so I didn't pick up".*

*Steve laughed. He said, "Vic, unless the Caller ID said 'GOD', you should never pick up during services".*

*I laughed nervously. After all, while it was customary for Steve to call during the week upset about something, it was unusual for him to call me on Sunday and ask me to call his home. I wondered what was so important?*

*"So Vic, we have an urgent issue, one that I need addressed right away. I've already assigned someone from my team to help you, and I hope you can fix this tomorrow" said Steve. "I've been looking at the Google logo on the iPhone and I'm not happy with the icon. The second O in Google doesn't have the right yellow gradient. It's just wrong and I'm going to have Greg fix it tomorrow. Is that okay with you?"*

Even as CEO of one of the worlds largest companies, Jobs had the attention to detail to still worry about even the littlest of things. Including the fact that the second 'O' in the Google icon wasn't quite the right gradient of yellow. Gundotra continues:

*But in the end, when I think about leadership, passion and attention to detail, I think back to the call I received from Steve Jobs on a Sunday morning in January. It was a lesson I'll never forget. CEOs should care about details. Even shades of yellow. On a Sunday.*

Rest in peace Steve Jobs.

Thanks for checking out my book. I hope you found this of value and enjoyed it. But before you go, I have one small favor to ask…

**Would you take 60 seconds and write a quick blurb about this book on Amazon?**

Reviews are the best way for independent authors (like me) to get noticed, sell more books, and it gives me the motivation to continue producing. I also read every review and use the feedback to write future revisions – and even future books. Thanks again.

Printed in Great Britain
by Amazon

49335778R00040